OPEN SESAME
English as a Second Language Series

ERNIE AND BERT'S
RED BOOK

Children's Television Workshop

Authors

Maureen Harris

Jane Zion Brauer

Illustrators

Tom Brannon

Mary Grace Eubank

Anne Sikorski

Photographer

Caroline Monaghan

Oxford University Press

Oxford University Press

200 Madison Avenue
New York, NY 10016 USA

Walton Street
Oxford OX2 6DP England

OXFORD is a trademark of
Oxford University Press.

Library of Congress Cataloging-in-Publication
Data

Zion, Jane S.
    Ernie and Bert's red book; featuring Jim
Henson's Sesame Street Muppets.
    (Open Sesame; stage F)
    Summary: Designed for Non-English speak-
ing children to help them develop listening
and speaking skills through conversations,
songs, chants, stories, and games accom-
panied by illustrations and photographs
featuring various Muppet characters.
    1. English language—Textbooks for foreign
speakers—Juvenile literature. [1. English
language—Textbooks for foreign speakers]
I. Brannon, Tom, ill. II. Eubank, Mary
Grace, ill. III. Sikorski, Anne, ill. IV.
Children's Television Workshop. V. Title.
VI. Series.

PE1128.Z56 1987   428.3′4   86-18038
ISBN 0-19-434164-X

The publisher would like to thank the follow-
ing for their participation in the photography
sessions:
Students and teachers of Netherwood Elemen-
tary School at Netherwood Road, Hyde Park,
New York; Ezra and Lauren Martin; Sylvia
McLemore; Peg Munves; Hernando Sanchez;
April Okano.

The publisher would like to thank the follow-
ing for permission to reproduce photographs:
Baldev/Sygma; Halley Ganges; R. Joedecke—
The Image Bank; Robert Phillips—The
Image Bank; Guido Alberto Rossi—The
Image Bank; Michael Salas—The Image
Bank; Al Satterwhite—The Image Bank;
John Lewis Stage—The Image Bank; Pete
Turner—The Image Bank; WIDE WORLD
PHOTOS.

The publisher would like to thank Tom
Cooke for permission to reproduce the
Sesame Street characters on the inside
front and back covers.

The following were reprinted by permission:
Excerpts from "I AM A MAN Ode to
Martin Luther King, Jr."
Copyright © 1971 by Eve Merriam. All rights
reserved. Reprinted by permission of Marian
Reiner for the author.

"Escondido" by Joe Raposo
© 1973 JONICO MUSIC, INC.
U.S. and Canadian Rights Administered by
Jonico Music, Inc. All Rights for the World
Outside the U.S. & Canada Administered by
APRIL MUSIC INC.
All Rights Reserved. International Copyright
Secured. Used by Permission.

"All Light Comes from the Sun" from *The
Man in the Moon: Sky Tales from Many Lands*
by Alta Jablow and Carl Withers. Holt,
Rinehart and Winston © 1969.

Printing (last digit): 9 8 7 6

Printed in Hong Kong

Developmental Editor: Debbie Sistino
Associate Editor: Lisa Ahlquist

PREFACE

Ernie and Bert's Red Book provides high-intermediate level students of English with information and practice in skills necessary for them to succeed in their content area classes. Lessons feature social studies, science, math, and cultural topics. Students also learn about using prefixes, suffixes, homonyms, the dictionary, the encyclopedia, charts, and maps.

The focus is on all four language skills. Children will develop their reading, writing, listening, and speaking abilities in English through stories, conversations, songs, chants, and poems all based on illustrations and photographs in the book. By the end of the *Red Book,* children are reading detailed stories, writing reports, and working in groups to make judgments about situations.

As in the other stages of Open Sesame, the curriculum moves from topic to function to structure. As stated above, the topics relate to subjects students are studying in their regular classes. The functions and structures reviewed and introduced are ones that help children convey information on the particular topics.

CONTENTS

Reach for the Rainbow

Reach for the rainbow
Rainbow, rainbow
It's right there in the sky
Right there in the sky
Reach for the rainbow
Rainbow, rainbow
Lift your arms high
High, high.

Over the rainbow
Rainbow, rainbow
You may have been told
May have been told
Over the rainbow
Rainbow, rainbow
Is a pot of gold
Pot of gold.

Now—reach for the rainbow
Rainbow, rainbow
Your wishes can come true
Wishes can come true
The magic of the rainbow
Rainbow, rainbow
Is inside me and you
Inside me and you.

ERNIE: Bert, what do you think is over the rainbow?

BERT: Not now, Ernie. I have to clean the kitchen.

ERNIE: Maybe there are mountains of bottle caps. Imagine, Bert. If you were over the rainbow, you could have mountains of bottle caps!

BERT: That would be nice. But I really should clean the kitchen now.

clouds filled with oatmeal

pigeons everywhere

BERT: Hey, neato! How do we get there?

BRUSH UP ON YOUR SKILLS

BERT: Have you ever seen a horsefly?

ERNIE: Sure, Bert. Yesterday I saw a horse fly over Sesame Street.

BERT: No, Ernie, not a horse fly, a horsefly.

ERNIE: I know, Bert. I was just kidding.

Compound Words

1. Match the words on the left with the words on the right to make compound words.

   Example: rain + bow = rainbow

foot	fly
pan	brush
birth	self
butter	day
my	ball
paint	cake

2. Now, write a sentence using each word. Then, draw a picture to go with each sentence.

   Example: What is over the rainbow?

MUMFORD: I want to show you a very special magic trick. This is a prism. It looks like a glass triangle. When light shines through a prism, look what happens!

GROVER: It looks like a rainbow!

MUMFORD: Right! A prism is like a raindrop. When the sun shines through the rain, we see a colorful rainbow.

GROVER: But the light from the sun is white.

MUMFORD: It looks white, but it really isn't. When the light shines through the rain, it bends and separates into colors. The colors we see are red, orange, yellow, green, blue, indigo, and violet.

4

What is over the rainbow?

Ask your friend:
1. What do you think is over the rainbow?
2. Who do you think lives there?
3. What might you do there?
4. How might it be different from where you live now?

Now write your friend's answers. Draw a picture to go with your paragraph.

The Robe of Feathers
A Folktale

This is a story about a fisherman named Yoshio. He lives alone on a small island in the Pacific Ocean.

One night there was a very bad storm. The next day the sun shone brightly. Yoshio wanted to see if his boat was all right, so he walked to the harbor. On his way he saw something hanging from a tree. It was a beautiful robe made of feathers. The feathers were all different colors, like a rainbow. They sparkled in the bright sun like jewels.

"I'll take this beautiful robe home," Yoshio said to himself. "I'll look at it whenever I'm lonely."

On his way home he saw a beautiful woman. She was crying. She stopped when she saw Yoshio.

"Oh, Mr. Fisherman," she said, "you found my robe of feathers." "I am a fairy," she explained. "I use the robe for wings. They got wet in the storm, so I put them on the tree to dry. If you don't give my wings back to me, I won't be able to fly."

Yoshio gave the fairy the robe of feathers. She was so happy she danced the fairy's dance. The robe of feathers sparkled in the sunlight. The island looked like it was wrapped in rainbows. Then the fairy flew away.

Yoshio is not lonely anymore. He has a beautiful memory to carry in his heart.

What would you do?

1. Karl went fishing and caught 32 fish. When he went to the market, he sold 25 fish. How many fish did he have left?

2. The next day, Karl caught a lot of fish. He got 4 boxes and put 20 fish in each one. How many fish did he catch altogether that day?

3. At the market, Karl bought potatoes for $.80 and other vegetables for $1.29. How much did he spend?

4. Karl found 9 crabs in the sand one morning. In the afternoon, he found 25 more. How many crabs did he find in all?

5. Karl wants to plant 25 trees in rows of 5. How many rows can he plant?

Listen to it

Listen to each paragraph and answer the question. Sometimes your answer will be true or false and sometimes your answer will be words or a sentence.

A 1. True or false: Sunlight is white.
   2. What are four colors of the rainbow?

B 3. True or false: A prism is like a raindrop.
   4. What does light look like when we shine it through a prism?

C 5. True or false: Ernie believes in rainbows.
   6. What makes Bert want to go over the rainbow?

D 7. True or false: Yoshio is poor.
   8. Where does Yoshio live?

E 9. True or false: Yoshio saw a robe in the sky.
  10. What was the robe made of?

Test your skill

These compound words are mixed up. Rearrange the different parts to form compound words that make sense.

footday   rainfly
toothball   butterlight
birthbow   mycake
sunbrush   panself

Write about it

Write one paragraph on your favorite color of the rainbow. Explain why it is your favorite.

The Magic of Magnets

Every magnet can attract
Most objects made of metal
Like paper clips, knives, forks,
and spoons
But not a flower petal.

Magnets, magnets, everywhere
We use them every day
In the kitchen or at school
And sometimes when we play.

GROVER: I wonder what this is.

BIFF: Oh, look, there's Grover.

SULLY: What are you doing with all our things?

GROVER: What things? Where did all these things come from?

BIFF: There's a magnet in your pocket. It attracts most objects made of metal, like our tools. Will you please give them back to us so we can return to work?

GROVER: Oh, I am so sorry!

SNUFFY: This magnet is fun to play with, Bird.
I wonder if it will attract a pencil.

BIG BIRD: No, Snuffy. A pencil isn't made of metal.

SNUFFY: Oh, that's right, Bird. I wonder if this
magnet will attract a nail.

BIG BIRD: Yes, Snuffy, it will. A nail is made of metal.

Bottom shelf:	Top shelf:
pencil	hammer
eraser	nail
crayon	screw
rubber band	wood
wooden ruler	saw
paper clip	tape measure
thumbtack	radio
paper	
notebook	

Measuring the Magnetic Field

A magnet has a force that can be felt in the area around it. This area is called the magnetic field. Choose a partner and do the following experiment to find out how the magetic field works.

Materials

- magnet
- paper clip
- piece of paper

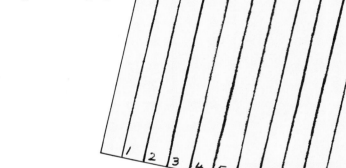

Procedure

1. Draw 12 lines on a sheet of paper. Make each line one inch apart. Number the lines.
2. Place a paper clip on one end of the paper.
3. Place a magnet on the other end of the paper.
4. Slowly move the magnet toward the paper clip.
   What happens when you get close to the paper clip? Do you feel anything?
5. Mark the place on the paper where the paper clip starts to move.
6. Repeat this three times. Each time, mark the place where the paper clip begins to move. Does it always begin to move in the same place?

Talk with your partner about what happened in the experiment.
Write the answers to the questions and present them to the class.

THIS IS

UN SAFE

Prefixes

A prefix is a syllable placed before a root word to change its meaning and form a new word.

1. The prefixes **un-** and **dis-** usually mean not.
    Example: Dishonest means not honest.
    Write a sentence with each of the following words. Then find the root word of each one.

unfair	disobey	unhappy
disagree	unsafe	

2. The prefix **re-** usually means again.
    Example: Repaint means paint again.

    Write a sentence with each of the following words. Then find the root word of each one.

reread	rebuild	refill
rewrite	redo	

3. Use the following words with prefixes to complete the paragraph.

unable	disobey	reread
unfair	unhappy	rewrite

    Betty Lou was very (1) _____ . She did her homework last night, but when she got to school she was (2) _____ to find it. Now her teacher told her she would have to (3) _____ the story and (4) _____ the report. Betty Lou thought this was (5) _____ , but she didn't want to (6) _____ her teacher. So she did her homework again. Can you guess where the missing homework paper was?

Read the story on the next two pages and see how many words with prefixes you can find!

15

Maggie from Magnesia

Many years ago, there was a sheep named Maggie. She lived in a little town called Magnesia. Maggie was no ordinary sheep. She wore bows on her ears and bells on her toes. She also kept her fleece coat in the latest style.

A shepherd named Sam was in charge of all the sheep in the pasture. He used a staff to keep them all together. This was not an easy job! All the sheep were very happy with Sam, except Maggie. She was very unhappy and bored in Magnesia. All the sheep liked the way Sam smiled at them, except Maggie. Maggie

disliked Sam's smile and thought he looked strange. All the sheep obeyed Sam's rules and stayed in the pasture, except Maggie. She disobeyed the rules and always wanted to run away. All the sheep in the pasture made Sam's job pleasant, except Maggie. She made his days very unpleasant.

One day Maggie disappeared. Sam was unable to find her. He was very worried. He took his staff and began looking for her in other pastures. Two days and two nights passed.

The next morning, Sam was still searching for Maggie. He wandered to

she could bring her friend with her, too. That made Maggie very happy. She was so pleased with her new friend and her new necklace that she redid the bows on her ears and fluffed up her coat. Then she followed Sam back to the old pasture.

Do you know the secret of the necklace? The tiny black objects are really magnets. Maggie is wearing magnets around her neck! Now Sam can use the metal tip of his staff to keep Maggie in the pasture. Make sure to keep it a secret! Maggie loves her new necklace and Sam hopes that Maggie will never try to disappear again.

another pasture. To his surprise, there was Maggie. She was not alone. Maggie had found another sheep who looked just like her. She had made a new friend. As Sam walked over to get Maggie, he noticed some tiny black objects on the ground. When he touched them with his staff, they stuck to the metal tip.

Sam had a great idea. He took the black objects and made a necklace out of them. When he saw Maggie, he told her he had a present for her. He gave her the necklace. He said that he had missed her very much and wanted her to rejoin the sheep in his pasture. He told her that

What was the argument about?
What could the students do to settle the argument?
What could the teacher do?

Materials

- magnet
- paper clips

Procedure

1. Make a pile of paper clips.
2. Dip your magnet into the pile and lift it up again.
3. Take the paper clips off, count them, and write down the number.
4. Repeat steps 2 and 3 two more times.
5. Add the three numbers together to get the total.
6. Divide the total by 3.

This final number is the average number of paper clips your magnet picked up from the pile.

If you can, try this experiment with different kinds of magnets: big, small, round, flat, bar, and horseshoe. What do you discover? What conclusions can you draw?

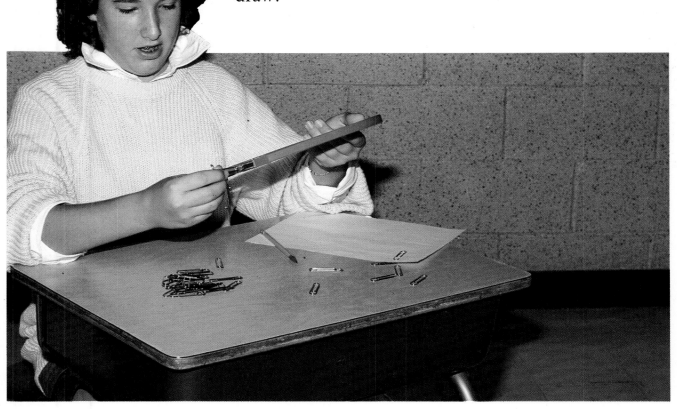

Listen to it

Listen to each paragraph and answer the questions. Sometimes your answer will be true or false and sometimes your answer will be words or a sentence.

A 1. True or false: Magnets attract paper.
   2. What are three things that magnets do not attract?

B 3. True or false: Grover found something interesting and put it in his bookbag.
   4. What was in Grover's pocket?

C 5. True or false: There were lots of metal objects in the Fix-It Shop.
   6. What are three things that a magnet would attract in the Fix-It Shop?

D 7. True or false: A magnetic field is a big space outdoors where you can play with magnets.
   8. Why can a magnet pull a metal object without touching it?

E 9. True or false: The Count's magnet picked up 21 paper clips altogether.

10. Why did the Count divide the total number of paper clips by 3?

Test your skill

Use the prefixes **un-**, **dis-**, and **re-** to make new words with the following root words. Then write a sentence using each new word.

certain   write   agree
sure   heat   obey

Write about it

Pretend you are a large magnet. Use the following questions to write a paragraph: What metal objects would you like to attract? Why?

Take Good Care of Yourself

Take good care of yourself.
Be healthy every day.
Exercise and eat good foods.
Energy's on its way.

Take good care of yourself.
Your health is up to you.
Brush your teeth, get plenty
    of sleep
And you will look good, too.

Take good care of yourself.
Each and every day.
Try to be happy and let it show.
A new friend may come
    your way.

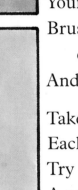

21

Fruit is delicious—
A treat that tastes great.
It's sweet and nutritious
And you don't need a plate.

Milk is a great snack
That's creamy and cool.
It's especially refreshing
Right after school.

Muffins for breakfast
Help start your day right.
Fresh from the oven
You'll love every bite.

We've talked about some foods
That you should eat each day
To be healthy and to grow.
Now you're on your way.

The Cat Stretch

Thousands of years ago, some people in India started a new form of exercise. They called it yoga. Today people still practice yoga because it is good for your body and it's fun to do.

Find a comfortable place on the floor. Here's how to do a yoga exercise called the cat stretch.

1. Lie on your stomach with your hands at your sides.
2. Place the palms of your hands next to each shoulder. Breathe in slowly as you push yourself up onto your knees.
3. Hold your breath as you slowly lower your bottom to your heels and your forehead to the floor. Stretch like a cat, from your shoulders to your fingertips. Breathe out.
4. Straighten up slowly. Bring your head up last.
5. Sit on your heels. Breathe deeply, in and out.

DENTIST: Hello, Mr. Silva. This is Dr. Allen. I am a dentist in the neighborhood. I would like to talk to your students about the importance of good dental care.

TEACHER: Oh, that would be wonderful! Come anytime!

DENTIST: How about Thursday, November first?

TEACHER: Oh, I'm sorry. We are going on a field trip that day.

DENTIST: Well, I see you have a very busy schedule, Mr. Silva. How about Tuesday, November twenty-seventh?

TEACHER: That will be fine. Come anytime on that day!

DENTIST: Are you sure?

TEACHER: Yes, that day is completely free!

NOVEMBER						
SUN	MON	TUES	WED	THUR	FRI	SAT
				Field Trip 1	2	3
4	Science Fair 5	6	7	8	9	10
11	12	School Play 13	14	15	Class Test 16	17
18	19	20	Thanksgiving Dance 21	22	23	24
25	26	(27)	28	29	30	

Listening to Your Pulse

The heart pumps blood out to the arteries. The arteries are tubes that carry blood to other parts of the body. Your pulse is the regular beat of the arteries caused by the pumping of the heart. Your pulse rate is the number of times your pulse beats in one minute. It is the same as your heart rate. You can feel your pulse at certain places on your body. These are the places where the arteries are closest to the surface. Your pulse feels strong when you are healthy and weak when you are sick.

Procedure

1. Run in place for 30 seconds.
2. Find your pulse point on the inside of your left wrist.
3. Put three fingers lightly on your pulse point.
4. Have your partner time you for 60 seconds.
5. Count how many times you feel a beat.
6. That number is your pulse rate. It is usually between 60 and 90 beats a minute.
7. Now change places with your partner. Time your partner for 60 seconds while he or she counts the pulse rate.

Would your pulse rate be slow or fast in the following situations?

☐ before you get out of bed in the morning

☐ after you do exercises for 15 minutes

☐ when you are sitting and relaxing

☐ when you feel excited

Discuss the answers with your partner and write them on a piece of paper. Share them with the class.

BRUSH UP ON YOUR SKILLS

Suffixes

A suffix is a letter or letters added to the end of a root word to change its meaning and form a new word.

1. Form new words by adding the suffix **-ly** and then write the correct words into the story below.

    bright   sudden   quick   friend

    One morning, the sun was shining (1) _____ in Prairie Dawn's window. She woke up (2) _____ and said, "Oh, no! I forgot to set my alarm clock and I'm late for school!" She got dressed (3) _____ and ran to the bus stop. The bus was still there. She was happy that she had such a patient and (4) _____ bus driver. She was also happy that she got to school on time.

2. Form new words by adding the suffix **-ful** and then write the correct words into the story below.

    use   care   pain

    Grover was playing outside with his friends during recess. By accident, he fell off of the jungle gym and hurt his knee. It was very (1) _____ . He went to the school nurse. The nurse washed his knee and put a bandage on it. The bandage was very (2) _____ because it helped his knee to heal. The nurse told him to be more (3) _____ next time.

3. The following words end with the suffix **-y**. Write the correct words into the story below. Can you figure out what the root words are?

    sunny   funny   tasty   icy

    It was a cold and (1) _____ afternoon in winter. Bert and Ernie were playing outside. They had a good time slipping and sliding on the (2) _____ sidewalks. They also built a (3) _____ looking snow monster. When they were too cold, they went inside and had hot chocolate and some (4) _____ cookies. What a nice afternoon!

Have you ever had a nightmare?
How did you get back to sleep?
How does not getting enough sleep affect your schoolwork?
What can you do to get a better night's sleep?

Calorie Chart

Food	Calories
1 apple	80
1 chocolate chip cookie	50
1 hamburger on a bun	365
1 hot dog	170
1 cup of ice cream	270
1 glass of lemonade	75
1 glass of milk	150
1 pear	100
1 slice of pizza	155

Look at what Betty Lou, Prairie Dawn, and Cookie Monster ate for lunch. Use the calorie chart to find out who had the most calories.

Betty Lou
  2 slices of pizza
  1 glass of lemonade
  1 apple

Prairie Dawn
  2 hot dogs
  1 glass of milk
  1 pear

Cookie Monster
  4 hamburgers on buns
  5 cups of ice cream
10 chocolate chip cookies

Listen to it

Listen to each paragraph and answer the questions. Sometimes your answer will be true or false and sometimes your answer will be words or a sentence.

A 1. True or false: Eating fruits and vegetables is a good way to be healthy.
2. What are three things you can do to be healthy?

B 3. True or false: Grover gave Cookie Monster a box of cookies.
4. What did Cookie Monster eat?

C 5. True or false: Samantha Jones has a toothache.
6. When will she see the dentist?

D 7. True or false: Your pulse rate is the same as your heart rate.
8. If you had the flu, how would your pulse feel?

E 9. True or false: Getting enough sleep is important to your health.
10. What are two things people do to get ready for a good night's sleep?

Test your skill

Use the suffixes **-ly**, **-ful**, and **-y** to form new words with the following root words. Then write a sentence using each new word.

cup   sure   dirt
slow   harm   cloud

Write about it

Use the following questions to write a paragraph about the things you do in your life to be healthy: What foods do you eat? What do you do for exercise? How often do you brush your teeth? How much sleep do you get at night? What do you do if you can't fall asleep? How do you feel about yourself?

UNIT 4

Stars

Stars, stars, stars at night
Made of gases, give off light
Stars, stars, stars at night
Size and color make them bright.
Stars, stars, stars at night
The hottest ones are blue-white.
Stars, stars, stars at night
The closest star is the sun—that's right.
Stars, stars, stars at night
Constellations are a beautiful sight.
Stars, stars, stars at night
Telescopes will bring them in sight.
Learn about stars and try as you might
To see the same stars the very next night!

31

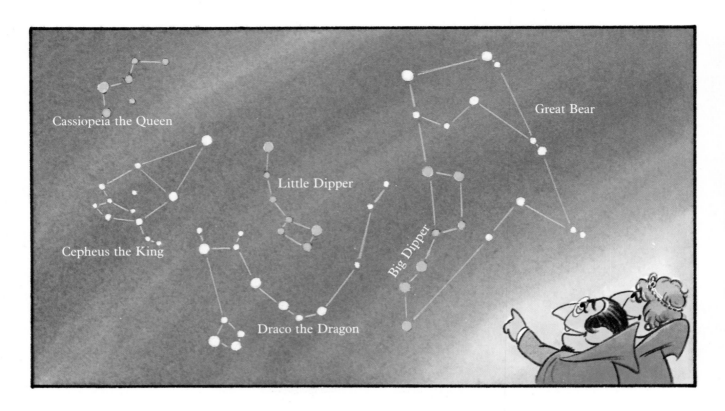

COUNT: What a wonderful night for counting stars: 1, 2, 3, 4, 5, 6, 7, 8, 9, 10.

COUNTESS: Oh, yes, and it's also perfect for finding constellations.

COUNT: ...11, 12, 13, 14, 15, 16, 17, 18, 19, 20.

COUNTESS: Did you know that a long time ago people gave names to these constellations? They named many of them after animals and people.

COUNT: ...21, 22, 23, 24, 25, 26, 27, 28, 29, 30.

COUNTESS: We still use those names because the constellations make the same pictures today.

COUNT: ...31, 32, 33, 34, 35, 36, 37, 38, 39, 40.

COUNTESS: Oh, look, I see the Big Dipper and the Little Dipper!

COUNT: ...41, 42, 43, 44, 45, 46, 47, 48, 49, 50.

COUNTESS: Now, I see Cassiopeia the Queen and Cepheus the King!

COUNT: ...51, 52, 53, 54, 55, 56, 57, 58, 59, 60.

COUNTESS: And I see some animals— the Great Bear and Draco the Dragon!

COUNT: ...61, 62, 63, 64, 65, 66, 67, 68, 69, 70.

COUNTESS: I'd love to know the stories behind these constellations, Count. Let's go to the library and find out more about them.

COUNT: Wonderful! We can go to the library right after I finish counting these stars: 71, 72, 73, 74, 75 . . . .

TELLY: Hello, I'm Telly, and I'm here at Sesame Street Science Center to interview Dr. Nobel Price. Dr. Price, is the sun a star?

DR. PRICE: Yes, of course it's a star.

TELLY: Why doesn't it look like other stars?

DR. PRICE: Because it's much closer to the earth than other stars.

TELLY: Oh, really? It's also much bigger than the other stars, isn't it?

DR. PRICE: No, it just looks bigger because it's so close to us.

TELLY: I see. But why does the sun look big and round and yellow? All the other stars look small and white.

DR. PRICE: The other stars look small and white because they're so far away. If they were all as close as the sun, or if we looked at them through a telescope, we would see that stars are different sizes and colors.

TELLY: That's amazing. Tell me more.

DR. PRICE: Well, all stars are very, very hot. The hottest stars are blue-white. Stars in the middle range are yellow. After that comes orange and then red. Red stars are the coolest of all, even though they are still very hot. So, since the sun is yellow, there are some stars that are hotter than the sun and some stars that are cooler. There are also some stars that are bigger than the sun and some stars

that are smaller. Our sun is a medium-sized star.

TELLY: I see. Is the sun very important for all of us?

DR. PRICE: Oh, yes, it's very important. Without the sun, the earth would be a cold and dark place. No one could live here.

TELLY: Thank you very much, Dr. Price. This is Telly at Sesame Street Science Center signing off.

How the Sun, Moon, and Stars Got into the Sky

A Myth

Once upon a time, a man named Nani and his daughter Keka lived in a forest in Africa. There was a famine and Nani went to hunt in the forest. While he was away, a mean dragon came and captured Keka. When Nani came back, the dragon captured him too, along with the deer he had caught. The dragon took Nani, Keka, and the deer and locked them all in his cave. They were surprised to find other people locked in the cave, too.

The people were afraid to escape, because of the mean dragon. When he was away, the dragon had a rooster watch over the cave. The rooster would crow loudly if someone tried to leave. But Keka was very smart, and soon she thought of a way to escape.

First, she found some grain and scattered it on the floor of the cave. This kept the rooster so busy eating that he couldn't crow. Next, she found some rope and made a strong ladder. Then she cooked the deer and gave it to the people to eat. They gave her the bones, which she put in a large bag.

Everything was ready. Keka threw one end of the ladder up to the sky. As if by magic, it landed on a cloud. One by one, the people began to climb. Keka stayed at the bottom.

Suddenly, the dragon returned, so Keka began to climb the ladder. She carried the bag of bones on her back. When the dragon got close to her, she threw down a bone and the dragon climbed down to eat it.

Keka finally reached the top of the ladder and climbed onto the cloud. Then she threw the ladder down and the mean dragon fell to the ground. Everyone was safe.

The people were so happy that their faces were shining. Now when you look up at the sky, you may think you see the sun, the moon, and the stars. But they are really the people who escaped from the dragon. Their faces are so bright they light up the sky!

Star light, star bright,
First star I see tonight,
Wish I may, wish I might
Have this wish I wish tonight.

What happened when Alicia and Roberto got home?

BRUSH UP ON YOUR SKILLS

ERNIE: Bert, I left the library today because the librarian said that I couldn't read in there.

BERT: What do you mean, Ernie? That's what a library is for.

ERNIE: She said, "No reading allowed."

BERT: She didn't mean "No reading allowed." She meant "No reading aloud."

ERNIE: Sounds the same to me!

Homophones

1. Homophones are words that sound alike but have different meanings and spellings. Here are some examples:

see	sea	red	read	weak	week
blew	blue	one	won	nose	knows
right	write	ate	eight	our	hour
meat	meet				

Use the homophones above to make 20 different sentences.

2. Can you think of any other homophones?

1. The Count and the Countess saw 5 constellations on Monday night. On Tuesday night they saw 7 constellations. On Wednesday night they saw 9 constellations. How many constellations did they see in all?

2. The 24 students in Ms. Kelly's class were learning about constellations. She told them that she wanted each student to study 3 different constellations. How many constellations did the whole class find out about?

3. Betty Lou was reading a book about stars. The book had 220 pages. It was divided into 11 chapters of equal length. How many pages were in each chapter?

4. The temperature on the surface of a yellow star is about 6,000°C. The temperature on the surface of a blue-white star is about 30,000°C. How many degrees hotter is a blue-white star than a yellow star?

TEST

Listen to it

Listen to each paragraph and answer the questions. Sometimes your answer will be true or false and sometimes your answer will be words or a sentence.

A 1. True or false: A star is made of gas.

2. Why do stars seem to move?

B 3. True or false: Our sun is a very large star.

4. Why does the sun look bigger than other stars?

C 5. True or false: Some constellations look like animals.

6. What are the names of three constellations?

D 7. True or false: The word *wish* occurs four times in the poem.

8. What are three words that rhyme in the poem?

E 9. True or false: Roberto and Alicia's parents called the police.

10. Who goes stargazing now?

Test your skill

Rewrite the following paragraph, using the correct homophones.

(*One, Won*) night last (*weak, week*), Grover, Betty Lou, and Cookie Monster went stargazing. The sky was no longer (*blew, blue*). It was very dark. They saw many, many stars shining above. Grover could (*see, sea*) some stars that were in the shape of a bear. "Who (*nose, knows*) the name of that constellation?" he asked. "I do," replied Betty Lou. "It's called the Great Bear."
"You're (*write, right*)," said Grover. "We (*read, red*) about it in school yesterday."

They saw (*eight, ate*) constellations in all that night. They watched the stars for one (*our, hour*). Then Cookie Monster got hungry. So he left to find a snack. The others decided they would (*meet, meat*) him later.

Write about it

Draw your own constellation. Make up a name for it and write a paragraph about it.

UNIT 5

REVIEW TEST 1

A. Listen and choose **a**, **b**, or **c**.

1.
    a    **b**    **c**

2.
    a    **b** 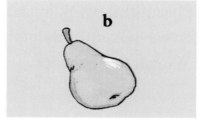   **c**

B. Listen and choose **a**, **b**, or **c**.

3. Grover hurt his _____ .
    a. elbow **b.** head **c.** knee

4. He _____ the jungle gym.
    a. climbed on **b.** fell off **c.** sat on

5. The _____ gave him a bandage.
    a. nurse **b.** dentist **c.** teacher

6. She told him to be more _____ next time.
    a. useful **b.** careful **c.** helpful

C. Listen and answer true or false.

7. Forgetful Jones went to the movies.

8. Betty Lou wanted milk and cheese.

9. She gave him two dollars.

10. Forgetful Jones found the money in his pocket.

REVIEW TEST 2

Read the paragraph and complete the sentences.
Choose **a**, **b**, or **c**.

When you look up at the sky on a clear night, you
see many tiny, twinkling lights. These are stars. Stars
are really very large but they are also very far away
from us. This is why they look so small. They are made
of gases and gases give off light. Stars come in many
sizes and colors. The hottest stars are blue-white. The
star closest to the earth is the sun. It is so close and
shines so brightly that in the daytime we can't see the
other stars. We can see all the beautiful, twinkling stars
only at night. Sometimes when we look up at the stars,
we can see shapes in the sky. We call these shapes
constellations.

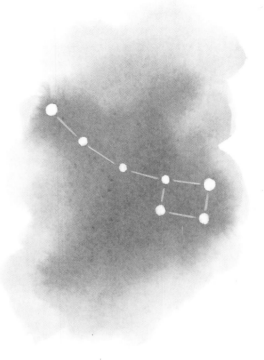

1. Stars look very tiny because _____ .
   a. they are tiny lights
   b. they are very far away from the
   earth
   c. they are made of gases

2. Stars are made of _____ .
   a. gases **b.** light **c.** heat

3. Stars give off _____ .
   a. gases **b.** light **c.** electricity

4. The sun is the brightest star we see
   because _____ .
   a. it is bigger than any other star
   b. it is hotter than any other star
   c. it is closer to the earth than any
   other star

5. Stars come in many different _____ .
   a. sizes and colors

   b. families and sizes
   c. colors and constellations

6. We can't see stars in the daytime
   because _____ .
   a. it's cloudy
   b. the sun is shining
   c. they're so far away

7. The constellation in the picture
   is _____ .
   a. Draco the Dragon
   b. Cepheus the King
   c. the Little Dipper

8. The best name for this story
   is _____ .
   a. All About Stars
   b. The Sun Is Bright
   c. Stars Twinkle at Night

REVIEW TEST 3

Read the paragraph and answer the questions.

Hi, my name is Grover. I am very special. You are very special, too. Remember, it is your responsibility to take good care of yourself. When you take good care of your body, you feel wonderful. I take good care of my body. I eat good food and get lots of rest. I exercise every day. When I am sick, I go to the doctor. I go to the doctor for regular check-ups, too. When I have a problem, I talk to someone about it. That always makes me feel better. When I am healthy, I feel happy. And I have lots of energy, too. Oh, I am so proud!

1. Who takes care of Grover?
2. Who is responsible for your body?
3. Why is it important to take good care of yourself?
4. When does Grover go to the doctor?
5. What does Grover do when he has a problem?

6. What is Grover eating in the picture?
7. What are three other things in the picture that are good for you to eat?
8. What is a good title for this paragraph?

REVIEW TEST 4

Read both stories. Fill in the missing word in each blank.

The Robe of Feathers

Yoshio the fisherman lived alone on a small island in the Pacific Ocean. One night there was a very (1) _____ storm. The next day the (2) _____ shone brightly. Yoshio wanted to (3) _____ if his boat was all right. So (4) _____ walked to the harbor. On his (5) _____ he saw something hanging from a (6) _____ . It was a beautiful robe made (7) _____ feathers. The feathers were all different (8) _____ , like a rainbow. They sparkled in the bright sun like jewels.

Maggie from Magnesia

A shepherd named Sam was in charge of all the sheep in the pasture. He used a staff to keep the (9) _____ all together. This was not an (10) _____ job! All the sheep were very (11) _____ with Sam, except Maggie. She was (12) _____ unhappy and bored in Magnesia. (13) _____ the sheep liked the way Sam (14) _____ at them, except Maggie. Maggie (15) _____ Sam's smile and thought he looked (16) _____ . All the sheep obeyed Sam's rules (17) _____ stayed in the pasture, except Maggie. (18) _____ disobeyed the rules and always wanted (19) _____ run away. All the sheep in (20) _____ pasture made Sam's job pleasant, *except* Maggie. She made his days very unpleasant.

REVIEW TEST 5

A. The following sentences are not in proper order.
    Read them and place them in order.

    1. Put three fingers lightly on your pulse point.
    2. Count how many times you feel a beat.
    3. Run in place for 30 seconds.
    4. Have your partner time you for 60 seconds.
    5. Find your pulse point on the inside of your left
        wrist.

B. Look at the pictures. Write a story about them.
    Make sure you have a beginning, a middle, and an
    end. Title your story "Grover's Mysterious Magnet."

Round and Round

Swing your hips
Round and round.
Touch your hands right to the ground.
Left knee up,
Left foot out.
Dance, dance, dance all about!

UNIT 6

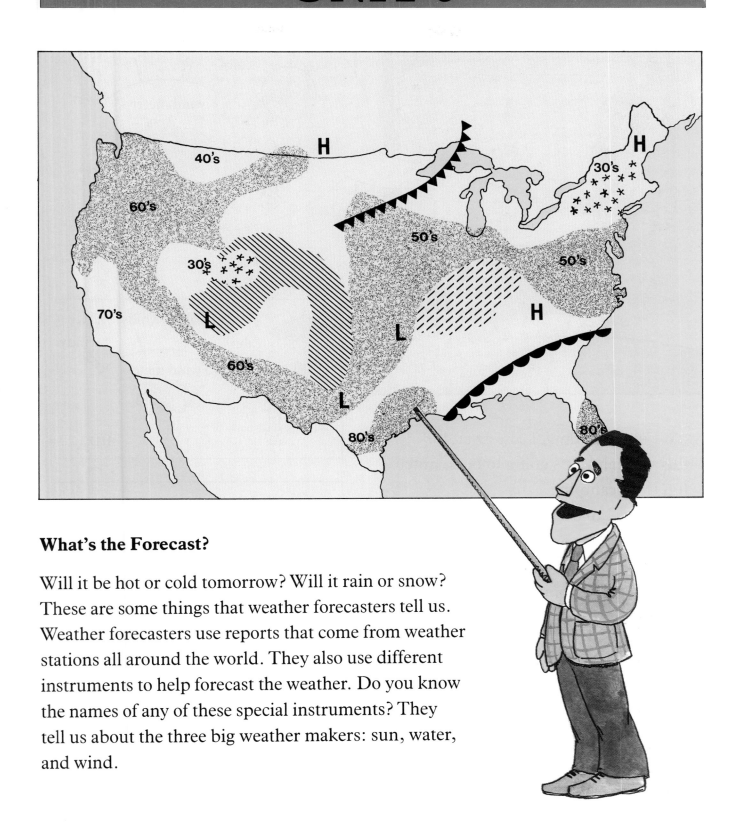

What's the Forecast?

Will it be hot or cold tomorrow? Will it rain or snow? These are some things that weather forecasters tell us. Weather forecasters use reports that come from weather stations all around the world. They also use different instruments to help forecast the weather. Do you know the names of any of these special instruments? They tell us about the three big weather makers: sun, water, and wind.

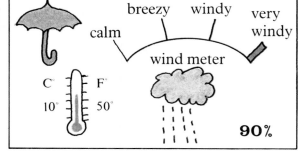

GROVER: Mommy, I can't wait for this weekend. It's going to be so much fun to go camping!

MOMMY: I'm excited, too. Let's listen to the weather forecast to find out what the weather will be.

GUY SMILEY: Tomorrow will be sunny and breezy. The temperature will be near seventy. There is a ten percent chance of rain.

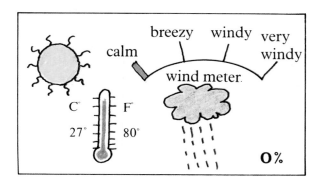

What should they do?

| Stratus Clouds | Cirrus Clouds | Cumulus Clouds |

Clouds

Three kinds of clouds, three kinds of clouds.
Each has a name, each has a name.
Stratus are flat and gray as the night.
Cirrus are curls of smoke in our sight.
Cumulus are fluffy and white.
Three kinds of clouds, three kinds of clouds.

Three kinds of clouds, three kinds of clouds.
Each is a sign, each is a sign.
Stratus tell us of rain in the sky.
Cirrus say weather will change in time.
Cumulus tell us the day will be fine.
Three kinds of clouds, three kinds of clouds.

The Water Cycle

Most of the earth is covered by water. The water is moving from one place to another all the time. This movement is called the water cycle. Here is how it works: The sun heats the water on the earth and the water rises into the air. The water becomes a gas called water vapor. This process is known as *evaporation*. When the water vapor cools, it becomes a liquid again. This process is called *condensation*. Clouds form when there is a lot of water in the air. Water falls back to the earth when the clouds become too heavy. This process is called *precipitation*. Precipitation can be rain or snow. Now the water cycle is complete. It begins over and over again.

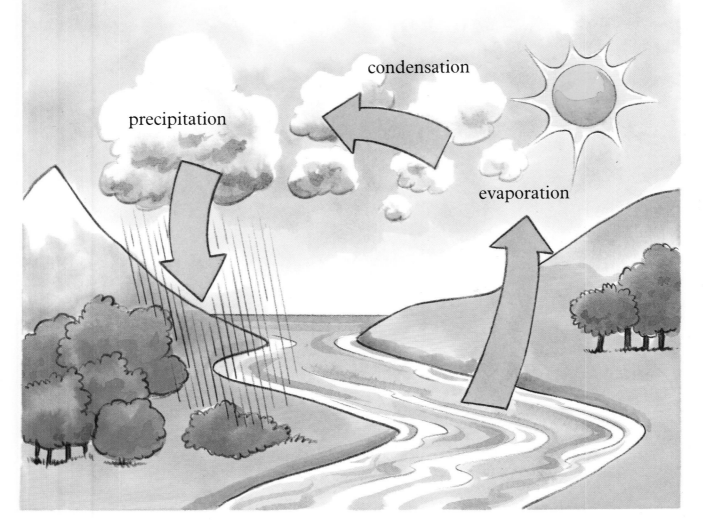

Let's look up the word *pigeon!*

Using the Dictionary

1. We use alphabetical order for many reasons. One important reason is to find words in the dictionary. Put the following words in alphabetical order:
    cloud   fog   rain   hail   breezy   pigeon

2. The two words printed in large or dark type at the top of a dictionary page are called *guide words*. The first guide word tells which word is first on that page. The second guide word tells which word is last on that page. These guide words help us use the dictionary more easily because we don't have to look at all the words on the page.

    Find the guide words that appear on the page of the dictionary for the words you put in alphabetical order above.

3. A *definition* tells what a word means. Some words have more than one definition. Use a dictionary to find the complete definitions of the following words:
    weather   forecast   constellation   hurricane

This experiment will help you observe how water moves through the water cycle. Choose a partner and do the experiment together.

Materials

- large jar
- hot water
- ruler
- aluminum foil
- ice cubes

Procedure

1. Fill the jar halfway with hot water.
2. Use a ruler to measure the level of the water. Write it down.
3. Place the aluminum foil over the opening of the jar.
   Press the foil lightly to make a bowl shape.
4. Put two or three ice cubes on top of the foil. Wait ten minutes.
5. Take off the aluminum foil carefully. Observe the bottom of the foil and the jar.
6. Measure and record the level of water again.

With your partner, write down the changes you observed during the experiment. Answer the following questions and share the answers with the class.

1. What did you observe when you measured the water level the second time?
2. Where do you think the water went? Why?
3. What do you think the ice did to the air in the jar?
4. What was on the bottom of the foil when you took it off the jar?
5. What parts of the water cycle did you see in this experiment?

A graph is a chart. It gives us information about changes that happen over a period of time. The graph on this page is called a bar graph. It shows us how the weather temperature changed during one week.

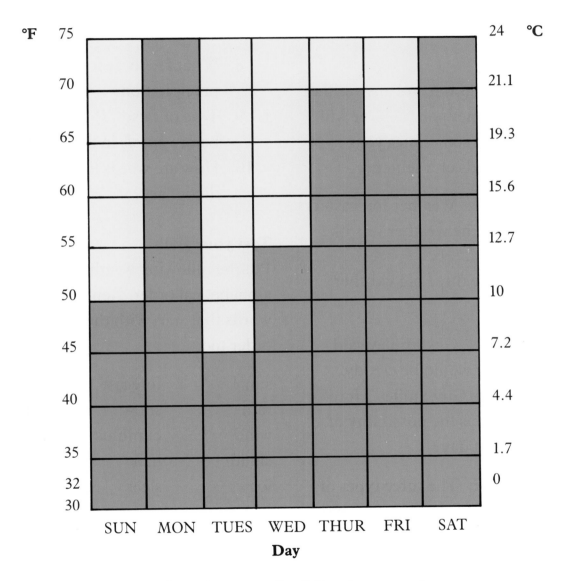

Look at the graph and answer the following questions:
1. Which day was the coldest?
2. Which day was the warmest?
3. Which two days had the same temperature?
4. What was the average temperature for the week?
   (Hint: Add the temperatures for the 7 days. Then divide by 7.)

55

Listen to it

Listen to each paragraph and answer the questions. Sometimes your answer will be true or false and sometimes your answer will be words or a sentence.

A 1. True or false: Weather forecasters tell us what the weather was like in the past.

2. What are the three big weather makers?

B 3. True or false: Guy Smiley said the next day would be cloudy.

4. According to Guy Smiley's forecast, what was the possibility of rain the next day?

C 5. True or false: The three types of clouds are cumulus, stratus, and cirrus.

6. What kinds of clouds do you see in the sky when it looks like it's going to rain?

D 7. True or false: When water condenses, it becomes a gas.

8. What are three forms of precipitation?

E 9. True or false: *Pigeon* comes before *puzzle* in the dictionary.

10. How are words listed in a dictionary?

Test your skill

Put the following weather words in alphabetical order. Remember to put words that start with the same letter in order too.

sun	forecast	stratus
rain	snow	cirrus
wind	cumulus	weather
cloud	hail	water
fog	sleet	cycle

Write about it

Use the following questions to write a paragraph about the weather: What is your favorite kind of weather? Why? What do you like to do in this kind of weather?

UNIT 7

The Environment

Look around at your environment—
Everything around you that you see.
There are houses, buildings, birds, and trees.
Air's all around for you to breathe.

People who live in your environment
Want to make it better every day.
Sometimes they are busy cleaning.
Other times they are building,
Making it nice for work and play.

57

Desert

Forest

City

Jungle

GROVER: Betty Lou! What are you doing in Jumping Jungle?

BETTY LOU: I'm looking for the treasure. Look at this map. I've followed the directions so far, but I still haven't found the treasure. The plants and birds are beautiful, though. And look at the cute little monkeys in that tree!

GROVER: I'm looking for the treasure, too. Let's look together. It says that we have to go through Daring Desert, Exciting City, Friendly Forest, Jumping Jungle, and Exotic Ocean. I've already been to Daring Desert and Exciting City. There was no treasure there. But I saw a camel in the desert. And I saw some palm trees. The city was exciting. There were so many people. There were enormous skyscrapers, too.

BETTY LOU: I've already been to Friendly Forest. I saw a family of deer, and the trees smelled wonderful. But I couldn't find the treasure.

GROVER: All that's left is Exotic Ocean.

GROVER and BETTY LOU: O.K. We're off!

BETTY LOU: Do you see anything, Grover?

GROVER: Not exactly. But look over there! There's a whale. And some beautiful shells are scattered on the beach. Do you want to know something, Betty Lou? I think the treasure has been all around us. Every place has been so beautiful. The treasure must be seeing all these beautiful places.

BETTY LOU: I think you're right. Let's go back to Sesame Street and tell everyone about the treasures we saw.

Ocean

The Pond in the Forest

Once upon a time, there was a little pond in the forest. Insects, frogs, turtles, fish, birds, and beavers lived there. They had been living together happily for a long time. The frogs made their homes by the lily pads, and the beavers built dams with the logs they found nearby. The sun gave energy to the plants and animals at the pond. It was a very happy environment. Rodeo Rosie, Prairie Dawn, Bert, and Ernie visited this pond every summer on weekends. They would go fishing in their rowboat, go swimming, take walks in the forest, and just relax as they listened to the crickets and the birds sing their songs. At night they would stay in a cabin nearby. They would play cards, read, play checkers, tell jokes, or just sit and talk together. What a wonderful and peaceful place to be!

Prairie Dawn, Bert, Ernie, and Rodeo Rosie returned to the pond this summer. They went to their cabin. But something was different. There was a factory next to it. When they went outside to sit by the pond, everything seemed different. Instead of the beautiful sounds of birds and crickets, they heard machines whirring. Instead of frogs hopping from lily pad to lily pad, they saw dirty water.

During the winter, some businesspeople had built a factory next to the pond. Chemicals from the factory emptied into the pond. The plants got sick from the chemicals. The insects couldn't eat the plants or drink the water or they would get sick, too. All the animals at the pond were very sad. This was their home, and now they had to leave.

Life at the pond was quiet and sad. What had happened to their beautiful place?

Your environment is everything around you. It's the place where you live and the places you go to every day. There are many people in your environment: parents, brothers, sisters, friends, teachers, librarians, crossing guards, and so on. When you talk with and live with these people each day, you interact with them. The way in which you interact with people changes how you feel about your environment.

One very important part of your environment is your home. Ask your partner:

1. What does your home look like?
2. Who lives at home with you?
3. How do you get along with the different people in your family?

4. What do you like most about your home?
5. What do you like least about it?
6. How do you feel when you are at home?
7. If you could make some changes in your home, what would they be?
8. If you could move to a new home, where would it be? What would it look like? Who would live there?

Write down your partner's answers. Now draw pictures of your partner's home now and the home he or she would like to live in.

Where should we build the road?

ERNIE: Gee, Bert. Look at the newspaper! It says here that the Nord Corporation is going to build a large office building at 85th Avenue and Pine Street.

BERT: I can't talk to you. I'm doing a crossword puzzle.

ERNIE: But Bert! Do you know where that is?

BERT: No, Ernie. Where is it?

ERNIE: That's at Pigeon Park! If they build that building there, we won't be able to play in the park anymore!

BERT: Oh, no! Pigeon Park! We must do something to save Pigeon Park!

ERNIE: What should we do?

BERT: I know. We should write a letter to the public officials. We should tell them that the park is important to the neighborhood.

ERNIE: Let's write the letter. Where should we begin?

BERT: That's easy. There are five parts.

1. The *heading* tells the date.
2. The *greeting* says hello to the person you're writing to.
3. The *body* tells all the things you want to say to that person.
4. The *closing* has a special word to say good-bye to the person.
5. You sign your name at the bottom. That's the *signature*.

ERNIE: That sounds easy. Let's write the letter!

BERT: O.K.

Here is Bert and Ernie's letter. Read it and find the heading, the greeting, the body, the closing, and the signature.

April 12

Dear Public Officials,

We have been playing at Pigeon Park since we were very little. We go there every day after school. In the summer we swim in the pool and go on the swings. In the fall we play football and soccer. In the winter we build snowmen, feed the pigeons, and ride sleds. In the spring we fly kites and play baseball. If you let the Nord Corporation put up a building there, we won't have anywhere to play. We'll be very sad.

Please save Pigeon Park. Build the office building somewhere else. Thank you for reading this letter.

Sincerely,

Bert and Ernie

Bert and Ernie

Listen to it

Listen to each paragraph and answer the questions. Sometimes your answer will be true or false and sometimes your answer will be words or a sentence.

A 1. True or false: There are many people in your environment.
   2. What does an environment include?

B 3. True or false: Betty Lou and Grover visited a farm.
   4. What was the treasure they found?

C 5. True or false: The chemicals from the factory were good for the animals.
   6. Why did the animals have to leave their home?

D 7. True or false: Frank loves his family.
   8. How does Frank relax?

E 9. True or false: Bert and Ernie got a letter from the Nord Corporation.
   10. Why will everyone be happy?

Test your skill

The following letter is mixed up. Put the five parts in the correct order and label them.

Your friend,
Thanks for the great idea you gave us to help our neighborhood. We now have a Sidewalk Patrol. Our neighborhood is cleaner than it has ever been and people are throwing less trash on the ground. Let's spread the word and keep up the good work!
Dear Betty Lou,
March 20
Rodeo Rosie

Write about it

Write a letter to a friend, to a relative, or to a public official about a problem. Don't forget all the parts of the letter!

UNIT 8

People

There are people in the world
Who have done special things,
Who have taught us all to lead better lives.

We write about these people
And we talk about them too,
To remember what it was they did or said.

Some created new machines.
Some set new records in sports.
Others wrote beautiful music.

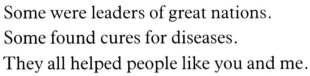

Some were leaders of great nations.
Some found cures for diseases.
They all helped people like you and me.

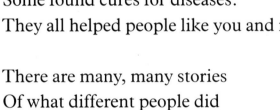

There are many, many stories
Of what different people did
To make the world a better place to be.

When you learn about these people
You'll learn about yourself,
And what it is you might have to give.

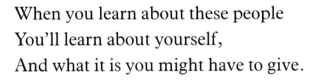

When you let yourself find out
What it is you like to do
You might find you do it better than
   the rest.

I AM A MAN: Ode to Martin Luther King, Jr.

Two seeking shelter entered inside:
room for them both, yet one was denied.

Two hungry men with money to pay:
one was served food, one turned away.

Two on the bus riding in town:
only one was allowed to sit down.

"I am a man," a young preacher said.

"I am no better than my brother,
"but I am no less than any other.

"Where the laws are unfair, it is right to resist.
"But not with a gun or an angry fist."

A peaceful army arose in the land.
Hand linked with hand, they took their stand.

"Fight to be equal, fight to be free,
"But only fight nonviolently."

"I have a dream," said the man with no gun,
"of equality for everyone,
"of an end to war and poverty.

"The poor are a mighty family.
"Brothers and sisters join with me."

EVE MERRIAM

BETTY LOU: Grover, I was just reading about Dr. Sally Ride, the first American woman to fly in space. Why don't you interview me and I'll pretend I'm Sally? Then I can tell you all about what I read.

GROVER: O.K., Betty Lou — I mean, Dr. Ride. What did you like to do when you were little?

"SALLY":   When I was little, I loved to read science fiction books. I also loved football, baseball, and tennis.

GROVER: How did you become an astronaut?

"SALLY":   I went to college and studied science. I got very good grades. One day I saw an announcement in my college newspaper for a job as an astronaut. I applied for the job. So did 9,000 other people. I was chosen! They said I was selected because of my background and because I'm able to learn things quickly.

GROVER: How did you feel when you were chosen?

"SALLY":   I felt so excited! I thought, "I can't believe I'm going to do this!"

GROVER: What did you do to prepare for your space flight?

"SALLY":   I had to study a great deal to learn how to work the panel control inside the spacecraft. I had to practice in a simulator, a machine that makes you feel like you are flying in space. I had to learn what to do in case we had any problems in flight. I also had to practice moving in a weightless environment. It took five years to prepare for my space flight!

GROVER: When and where did you lift off?

"SALLY":   My space shuttle, the *Challenger*, lifted off at Cape Canaveral, Florida, at 7:33 A.M. on June 18, 1983.

GROVER: How did it feel being in the *Challenger*?

"SALLY":   The thing I remember most about the flight is that it was fun. In fact, I'm sure it was the most fun I ever had.

GROVER: Thank you, Dr. Ride. Back to you, Betty Lou.

BETTY LOU: Gee thanks, Grover. For a moment I felt I really was Sally Ride! Being an astronaut sounds so exciting. Do you think Dr. Price could build me a simulator?

69

José Feliciano is a famous singer and songwriter. He was born in 1945 in Lares, Puerto Rico, where his father was a farmer. He was the second of twelve children. When he was a young boy, he and his family moved to Spanish Harlem in New York, but he never forgot his home in Puerto Rico.

He taught himself how to play the guitar and the accordion. He was born blind. It's true that he has never seen any of the things he writes about, but he hears things very clearly.

As a singer, he travels around the world giving concerts so that people can enjoy his music. He returns to Puerto Rico often. He has always thought of Puerto Rico as his home. One of his favorite songs describes how he feels about living in New York City and how he dreams of going back to Puerto Rico. The first part goes like this:

In the summertime, the city steams
With the kind of heat that can melt my
    dreams.
Though the times are hard, still I work
    and stay,
But my mind takes me far away

To Puerto Rico. The sun's always warm
And the sky's like a crystal dome.
In Puerto Rico, the wind from the
    mountaintop sings to me.
'Cause Puerto Rico is my home.

Indira Gandhi was one of the most powerful leaders of her time. From 1966 to 1984, she was Prime Minister of India, a country with 700,000,000 people.

When Indira was young, India was not an independent country. It was ruled by Great Britain. Indira's family fought hard to make India free. They fought peacefully by not paying taxes to Great Britain, by not obeying unjust laws, and by not buying goods produced outside of India. Police from Great Britain put most of Indira's family in jail for not obeying the laws.

In 1947, after much struggle, India gained its independence. Indira's father became the first Prime Minister. Indira traveled everywhere with him. In 1966, two years after he died, Indira ran for Prime Minister and won. She was devoted to her people and tried to help the poor. She also worked hard to unite the many different social groups in India.

In 1984, Indira Gandhi was assassinated by a group of people who disagreed with her ideas. Nations around the world mourned her death.

Bruce Lee was born on November 27, 1940, in San Francisco. It was during the Chinese Year of the Dragon. He often got into street fights, but he lost many of them because he was so small. To improve his ability to defend himself, he began to learn karate.

Over the next few years, a remarkable thing happened. Bruce studied karate and it gave him the discipline he needed to focus his life in a positive way. The energy he once devoted to fighting on the streets he now devoted to improving his karate moves. As he became stronger, his confidence grew. He no longer had to prove he was better than the others. His goal now was to become a karate expert.

Bruce Lee gained worldwide fame for his skill in the martial arts. He became an actor and starred in television shows about karate. He also directed and acted in a number of karate movies.

After a while he opened a school of karate. The type of karate he invented and taught is called Jeet Kune Do. Only the most dedicated students were allowed to enter Bruce Lee's school. He loved teaching and always told his students to work hard, but to love the work they were doing. He wanted them to experience the joy of learning. This is the message that the "King of Karate" gave to the world.

1. Sally Ride was born in 1951. She lifted off into space on the space shuttle *Challenger* in 1983. How old was she when she took her first space flight?

2. José Feliciano was 23 years old when he made his first record album. He was born in 1945. In what year did he record his first album?

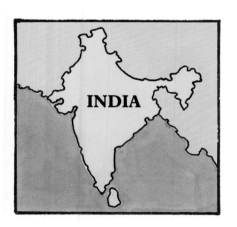

3. Indira Gandhi was born in 1917. She became Prime Minister of India in 1966. How old was she then?

4. Bruce Lee was 26 years old when he opened his karate school. He was born in 1940. In what year did he open this school?

74

ERNIE: Gee, Bert. What are you doing?

BERT: I'm writing an autobiography.

ERNIE: A what?

BERT: An autobiography.

ERNIE: What's an autobiography?

BERT: It's the story of my life.

ERNIE: Oh, so that's why you have all these pictures all over the table! You were so cute when you were little!

BERT: Do you really mean that, Ernie?

ERNIE: Sure, Bert.

Write your own autobiography. Here's how:

1. Get some index cards or small pieces of paper.
2. Write about a different time in your life on each piece of paper.
3. Put your ideas in the order in which they happened.
   Then attach them to a piece of string with paper clips.
4. Hang your string in the classroom. It will look like a clothesline of your life!
5. Write a paragraph about each idea. Use photographs, if you have them, to show what happened.

Share your story with the class!

TEST

Listen to it

Listen to each paragraph and answer the questions. Sometimes your answer will be true or false and sometimes your answer will be words or a sentence.

A 1. True or false: When you fight nonviolently, you use guns.
   2. What did the new laws do?
B 3. True or false: Sally Ride had to learn how to work a panel control.
   4. Why did she use a simulator?
C 5. True or false: José Feliciano's uncle taught him to play the guitar and the accordion.
   6. What did José Feliciano love as a boy?
D 7. True or false: When Indira Gandhi was young, India was a free country.
   8. What was one way the Indian people fought peacefully?
E 9. True or false: Bruce Lee was famous for being an expert boxer.
  10. How did Bruce Lee show his talent to the world?

Test your skill

These five short paragraphs about Sally Ride are out of order. Read them and organize them into a story.

1. I had to study a great deal for my first space flight. I had to practice in a simulator, a machine that makes you feel like you are flying in space. The simulator helped me learn what to do in case we had any problems in space.
2. When I was little, I loved to read science fiction books. I also loved sports like football, baseball, and tennis.
3. My space shuttle, the *Challenger*, lifted off at Cape Canaveral, Florida, at 7:33 A.M. on June 18, 1983.
4. When I got older, I went to college and studied science. One day, I saw an announcement in my college news-paper for a job as an astronaut. I applied for the job. So did 9,000 other people. I was very excited when they chose me!
5. The thing I'll remember most about my first flight is that it was fun. In fact, I'm sure it was the most fun I ever had.

Write about it

Think about your favorite relative: your father, mother, sister, brother, aunt, uncle, or grandparent. Write three para-graphs about this person's life. Make sure you have a beginning, a middle, and an end to your story.

UNIT 9

Hooray for People

Hooray for people, hooray for people,
On this big earth everywhere.
Hooray for people, hooray for people.
There is so much that we share.

People come from different places,
Cities, towns, and country spaces.
What we often do discover
Is how much we're like one another.

People speak in different styles.
Still we understand their smiles.
So what never can divide us
Are the feelings deep inside us.

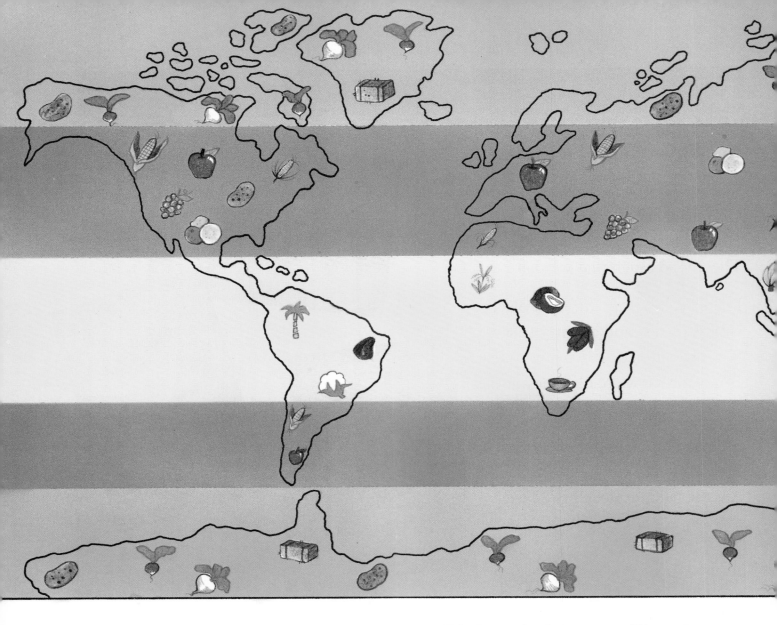

The World Is an Exciting Place

Different people live in different countries all over the world. They speak different languages, eat different kinds of food, and wear clothing suited to the weather in their country. When you travel to other countries, you realize that there are many new things to learn. You also discover that people all over the world have many similarities. We all share the same feelings deep in our hearts.

It's fun to look at maps. They give us information about many things. This map shows the different people, climates, and crops in the world. Countries near the equator have warm climates. As you move away from the equator, the climate becomes colder. Climate refers to the weather over a long period of time in one place. There are three basic climates on the earth. *Tropical* climates are found near the equator. *Temperate* climates are found farther

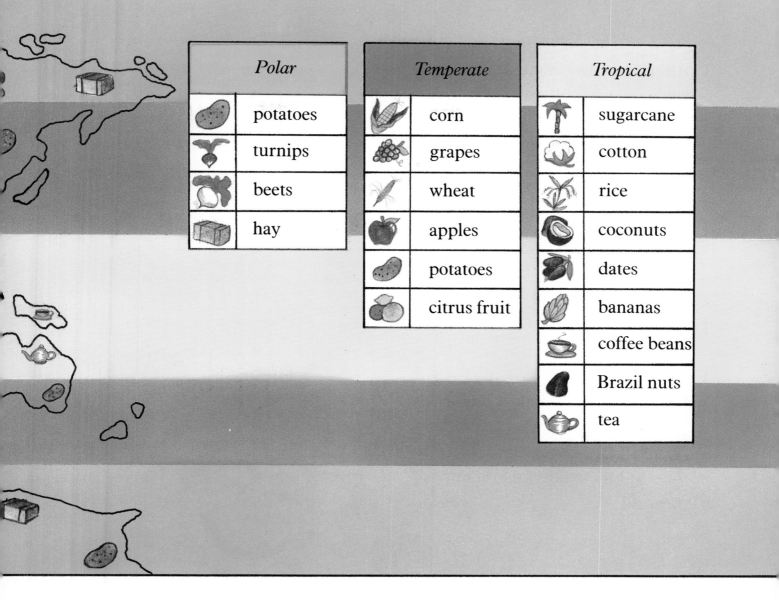

Polar		Temperate		Tropical	
	potatoes		corn		sugarcane
	turnips		grapes		cotton
	beets		wheat		rice
	hay		apples		coconuts
			potatoes		dates
			citrus fruit		bananas
					coffee beans
					Brazil nuts
					tea

away from the equator. *Polar* climates are found at the farthest points from the equator.

Different crops grow in different climates in the world. A long time ago, people ate only the food that grew in their own climate zone. Today, airplanes, boats, and trucks carry food from one climate to another so that we can enjoy it all!

Answer the questions about each climate zone. Use your map.

1. What color is this zone on your map?
2. Is it near or far from the equator?
3. What crops grow there?
4. What are some of the names of countries in this particular zone?
5. What kind of clothing do you think people wear in this climate zone?

COUNTESS: Darling, is it true that you've traveled all over the world?

COUNT: Yes, I have, dear Countess. I love counting the countries I've been to: 1, 2, 3, 4, 5, 6, 7, 8, 9, 10 . . . .

COUNTESS: Did you ever go to Brazil?

COUNT: Of course.

COUNTESS: Were you near the equator?

COUNT: Yes, I was.

COUNTESS: What crops did you see growing there?

COUNT: I saw 5,436 lovely cotton plants, 6,987 wonderful coffee bean plants, 3,296 delicious sugarcane plants, and 3,820 beautiful banana trees. It was wonderful to count them all!

ERNIE: Hey, Bert.

BERT: Yes, Ernie.

ERNIE: What's an encyclopedia? Is it some kind of large animal?

BERT: No, Ernie. It's a set of books that has information on many subjects.

ERNIE: Really? Like what?

BERT: The encyclopedia is organized alphabetically. So, for example, if you want to find out about pigeons, you would look under the letter **P**.

ERNIE: No, I wouldn't, Bert. If I needed some information about pigeons, I would ask you!

BERT: Oh, Ernie!

Use the encyclopedia. Look up the name of a country you're interested in and write a report answering the following questions:

1. What is the climate like?
2. What crops grow there?
3. What language do the people speak?
4. What interesting things might you see there?
5. What holidays do people celebrate there? Describe one.

Do you know why mice like to play on monkeys' noses?
Read this story and you'll find out!

Monkey See, Monkey Do

Once upon a time there was a family of monkeys that lived in the jungle. They enjoyed every day together. They ate bananas in the trees, swung from their tails, and took long afternoon naps.

But one monkey was very curious. Her name was Oogle. One day when her family was asleep, she went off to explore. She wandered into a field.

Oogle was very friendly and playful. She liked to copy what she saw others doing. When she saw a family of cats wagging their tails, she wagged her tail back at them. They had never seen a monkey before. Oogle looked different. The cats ignored her. So she went on.

Next, she saw a family of mice. They were busy building a house underground to get away from the cats. They had never seen a monkey before either. They were carrying bits of food in their

mouths, so Oogle put some things in her mouth and started walking next to the mice. When they saw what Oogle was doing, they got scared and ran underground very quickly. Now Oogle felt sad. The cats had ignored her and the mice were afraid of her.

Oogle got tired and decided to take a nap beside the mouse hole. While she was sleeping, she felt something tickle her nose. She opened her eyes and saw a mouse sitting on her nose. The mouse made a funny face at Oogle, so she made a funny face back at him. The mouse winked at Oogle, so she winked back. Then Oogle said, "Hi. My name's Oogle, and I'm a monkey. Who are you?"

"I'm Marty, and I'm a mouse," he said. "My family is scared of you, but I'm not. I wanted to meet you. Why haven't I seen any animals like you before?"

"I think it's because my family lives high in the trees. I came down here to go exploring. I love to meet new animals and see new places," said Oogle.

"While you were walking around down here, did you see any other animals?" asked Marty.

"Yes, I saw some animals that were brown and had four legs and long tails," answered Oogle.

"Really!" exclaimed Marty with fear. "Those are cats. They like to eat mice. We must be very careful of them. That is why we live underground in holes. Sometimes they find our holes and try to get us out of them. Do you think you could help us?"

"Maybe. What do you want me to do?" asked Oogle.

"Sit here and watch out for the cats. If you see them coming our way, bang your tail three times on the ground and then

sit on top of our hole," explained Marty. "That way they'll never find us, and maybe they'll go somewhere else looking for mice."

"That will be very easy to do," said Oogle, and that's just what she did.

Oogle stayed for a while and warned Marty and his family whenever danger was coming their way. Then she went back up into the trees and told her family about the friend she had made.

Oogle continued to visit Marty from time to time. Soon Oogle's brothers and sisters and Marty's brothers and sisters became friends. If you walk past the mouse hole on a day when the monkeys are visiting, you can see mice on the monkeys' noses. They will all be making funny faces and having a good time.

Isn't it wonderful that Oogle and Marty took the chance to become friends?

What might happen?
If you were a team captain, what would you do?

1. Maria was planting rows of sugarcane. She planted 9 plants in each row. She planted 13 rows. How many sugarcane plants did she plant?

2. Hai was picking bananas from a banana tree. He was going to sell the bananas at the market. He picked 35 bananas. There were 5 bananas in each bunch. How many bunches did he pick?

3. Heidi planted 64 apple trees. She planted 8 trees in each row. How many rows of apple trees did she plant?

4. The Count, Grover, and Bert were having a contest. They were trying to guess how many coffee beans were in the jar. Bert knew how many beans were in the jar because he put them in. He put 9 large spoonfuls of coffee beans into the jar. Each spoonful had 38 coffee beans in it. How many coffee beans did Bert put in the jar?

TEST

Listen to it

Listen to each paragraph and answer the questions. Sometimes your answer will be true or false and sometimes your answer will be words or a sentence.

A 1. True or false: There are many different languages in the world.

   2. What important thing do all people share?

B 3. True or false: It is cold in the polar zone.

   4. Why is it warm in the tropical zone?

C 5. True or false: Coconuts grow on Sesame Street.

   6. How is food brought from one country to another?

D 7. True or false: Oogle made friends with the cats.

   8. How did Oogle help Marty the Mouse?

E 9. True or false: Angela lives in a warm climate.

   10. Where does Angela's family go on picnics?

Test your skill

Complete these sentences with **a, b,** or **c.**

1. Apples grow in the _____ zone.
   a. tropical   **b.** temperate **c.** polar

2. Coconuts grow in the _____ zone.
   a. tropical   **b.** temperate **c.** polar

3. _____ grows in the temperate zone.
   a. Rice   **b.** Cotton   **c.** Corn

4. _____ grows in the tropical zone.
   a. Wheat   **b.** Sugarcane **c.** Hay

5. Beets grow in the _____ zone.
   a. tropical   **b.** temperate **c.** polar

Write about it

Write three paragraphs about your favorite holiday. In the first paragraph, tell the name of the holiday and why you celebrate it. In the second paragraph, tell what you do to get ready for the holiday. In the last paragraph, tell what you do on the holiday and why you like it.

UNIT 10

REVIEW TEST 6

A. Listen and choose **a, b,** or **c.**

1.   **a**   **b**   **c**

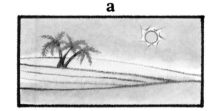  

2.   **a**   **b**   **c**

B. Listen and choose **a, b,** or **c.**

   3.   The Amazon Jungle is in _____ .
       a. Africa   **b.** South America   **c.** North America

   4.   Dr. Nobel Price saw _____ in the trees.
       a. monkeys   **b.** tall   **c.** coconuts

   5.   The Redwood _____ is in California.
       a. Desert   **b.** Jungle   **c.** Forest

   6.   The trees are so _____ you can't see their tops.
       a. red   **b.** tall   **c.** long

C. Listen and answer true or false.

   7.   Grover and Big Bird went to the beach.
   8.   The weather tomorrow will be hot.
   9.   The temperature will be between 60 and 65 degrees.
   10.   There is a 55 percent chance of rain.

REVIEW TEST 7

Read the story and complete the sentences. Choose **a, b,** or **c.**

One afternoon, Oscar was sitting in his trash can and looking up at the clouds. He had fun imagining many different things in the sky. One cloud looked like a Grouch Castle. Another cloud looked like a sardine and pickle sundae. Still another looked like a dragon. Oscar wondered what it would be like to live in Grouch Castle. How much fun it would be to be King of the Grouches! He could have all the yucchy things he wanted.

The clouds Oscar was looking at are called cumulus clouds. They are big, white, and fluffy. They forecast good weather. They have many shapes. Try Oscar's game sometime. What things can you see in the clouds?

1. The types of clouds Oscar was looking at are called _____ .
   a. cumulus   **b.** stratus   **c.** cirrus

2. These types of clouds forecast _____ .
   a. rain
   b. changing weather
   c. good weather

3. The clouds Oscar saw were _____ .
   a. big, white, and fluffy
   b. small, white, and fluffy
   c. big, black, and fluffy

4. To imagine means to _____ .
   a. help other people
   b. make up stories in your mind
   c. dream at night

5. When Oscar imagines, he can _____ .
   a. dance
   b. sing
   c. pretend to be anything he wants to be

6. One cloud was shaped like a _____ .
   a. trash can
   b. dragon
   c. banana peel

7. Oscar imagined he was _____ .
   a. living in Grouch Castle
   b. a sardine and pickle sundae
   c. a dragon

8. The best title for this story is _____ .
   a. King of the Grouches
   b. The Dragon and the Castle
   c. Fluffy White Clouds

REVIEW TEST 8

Look at the graph and answer the questions.

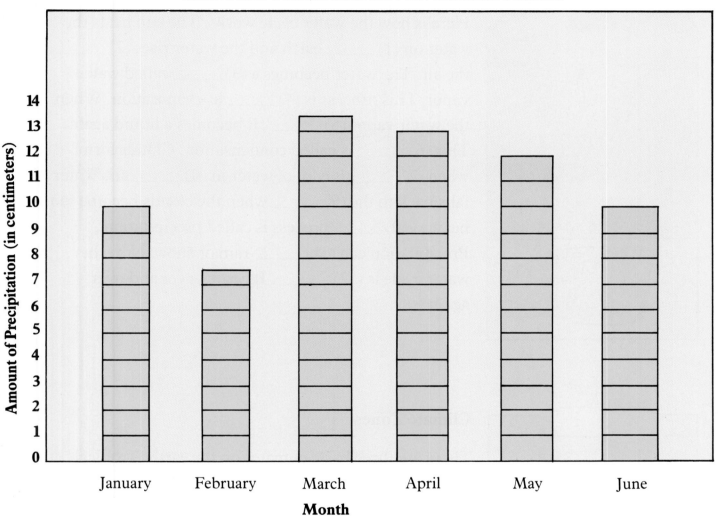

MONTHLY PRECIPITATION ON SESAME STREET

1. What month had the most precipitation?
2. What month had the least precipitation?
3. What two months had the same amount of precipitation?
4. How much more precipitation was there in April than in January?
5. What month had 7.5 cm of precipitation?
6. How many inches of precipitation fell in January? (Remember, 2.5 cm = 1 inch.)
7. How much precipitation fell in May?
8. What was the average amount of precipitation for January through June?

REVIEW TEST 9

Read both stories. Fill in the missing word in each blank.

The Water Cycle

Here is how the water cycle works. The sun heats the water on (1) _____ earth and the water rises (2) _____ the air. The water becomes a (3) _____ called water vapor. This process is (4) _____ as evaporation. When the water vapor (5) _____ , it becomes a liquid again. This (6) _____ is called condensation. Clouds form when (7) _____ is a lot of water in (8) _____ air. Water falls back to the (9) _____ when the clouds become too heavy. (10) _____ process is called precipitation. Precipitation can (11) _____ rain or snow. Now the water cycle is (12) _____ . It begins over and over again.

Climate Zones

There are three basic climates on the earth. Tropical climates are found near the (13) _____ . Temperate climates are found farther away (14) _____ the equator. Polar climates are found (15) _____ the farthest points from the equator. (16) _____ crops grow in different climates in (17) _____ world. A long time ago, people (18) _____ only the food that grew in (19) _____ own climate zone. Today, airplanes, boats, (20) _____ trucks carry food from one climate to another so that we can enjoy it all!

REVIEW TEST 10

A. The following paragraphs are not in proper order. Read them and place them in order.

Monkey See, Monkey Do

1. Oogle went to play in a field. She met a mouse. They played together and became good friends. The mouse asked her to help protect him from the cats in the field. Oogle said she would help.

2. Once upon a time there was a family of monkeys that lived in the jungle. They enjoyed every day together. They ate bananas in the trees, swung from their tails, and took long afternoon naps. But one monkey was very curious. Her name was Oogle. One day when her family was asleep, she went off to explore.

3. Oogle sat on top of the mouse hole. When the cats came near the hole, Oogle banged her tail three times. The mice knew that this was a warning and that they shouldn't come out of the hole. Then, Oogle went back and told her family what had happened. It was fun to make a new friend.

B. Look at the pictures. Write a story about them. Make sure you have a beginning, a middle, and an end. Title your story "A Factory Comes to Rolling River."

Last summer . . .

This spring . . .

This summer . . .

Smile

When you meet someone new
A smile will see you through.
S-M-I-L-E
S-M-I-L-E
S-M-I-L-E
A smile will see you through!